SONNETS ON LIFE

SWARNIKA

Copyright © Swarnika
All Rights Reserved.

ISBN 979-888606425-4

This book has been published with all efforts taken to make the material error-free after the consent of the author. However, the author and the publisher do not assume and hereby disclaim any liability to any party for any loss, damage, or disruption caused by errors or omissions, whether such errors or omissions result from negligence, accident, or any other cause.

While every effort has been made to avoid any mistake or omission, this publication is being sold on the condition and understanding that neither the author nor the publishers or printers would be liable in any manner to any person by reason of any mistake or omission in this publication or for any action taken or omitted to be taken or advice rendered or accepted on the basis of this work. For any defect in printing or binding the publishers will be liable only to replace the defective copy by another copy of this work then available.

Even without you noticing,

Life happened

And You Lived...

Contents

Contents

Preface

-Nishtha Trehan

"To live is the rarest thing in the world. Most people exist, that is all."

-Oscar Wilde

Life. Love. Grief. Growth. Fall. Joy. Gloom. Faith. Belief. Heartbreak. Loss. Disappointment. Expectation. Motivation. Inspiration. Regret. Guilt. Alone. Lonely. Solitude. Soliloquy. Empathy. War. Peace. Destination. Path. Blessing. Consumption. Destruction. Ruin. Damnation. Breath. Death. Honour. Betrayal. Forgiveness. Redemption. Soul. Relationships. People. Friends. Lovers. Family. I. We. Us.

A four-letter word, life, is ineffable. When asked to describe life, no two people can come up with the same definition. It is inexplicable, inscrutable, unprecedented and so, so, so temporarily permanent. An oxymoron, life is open to everyone's own interpretation. To limit life to one definition would be erroneous.

Watering your plants first thing in the morning? That's life. Covering your mother with a blanket when she has fallen asleep? That's life. Spending time and reading today's newspaper to your grandparents? That's life. Being there for your friends when they need you? That's life. Rereading your favourite book? That's life. That feeling of wanting to experience something (a moment, reading a book as if you're reading it for the first time, your firsts, etc.) all over again? That's life. Moving mountains just to be next to someone? That's life? Getting through the day even if that's the last thing you want? That's life. Forming new connections, meeting new people, smiling at strangers? That's life. Losing a loved one and moving on? That's life. Always, always, always moving forward? That's life.

Life is an experience different for everyone. It can be as short as seconds, minutes, hours, years or it can be as long as seconds, minutes, hours, and years. It is a loving, breathing thing that surrounds us everywhere. The opposite of life i.e. death is in fact the absence of life too.

In this collection Sonnets on Life, poets Swarnika, Deepanshi Ailawadi, Nishtha Trehan, Gauri Shukla, Khushi Kaushik, Putul Mangni Mandal, and Raman Singh have explored different aspects of life. With use of rhyming schemes such as 4(abab)+4(cdcd)+ 6(efefef), 5(ababc)+5(ababc)+4(abcc), and 4(abcb)+4(defe)+6(ghihjj), the poets have each written two sonnets that offer a homage to the classic Shakespearean and Petrarchan sonnet. With extraordinary clarity and a personalised touch, themes of healing, fear of loss and death, birth of a child, disillusion due to love, the transience of life, tyrannical society, unfinished poetry, the mundane of life and the circle of life have been expressed.

Acknowledgements

Sonnets On Life is a collection of poetry that has been uniquely designed. The collection is the result of a project taken up by Nrityangana Kala Kendra where each poet had to submit two sonnets each. Working on this anthology has been a wonderful experience, but it wouldn't have been the same without the dedication and contributions made by my fellow poets. I'd like to thank Gauri Shukla, Khushi Kaushik, Putul Mangni Mandal, Raman Singh, Deepanshi Ailawadi, and Nishtha Trehan for working on the sonnets present in this book and sharing them with our readers. They have written these sonnets beautifully and shared their insights on life through them.

Prologue

- *Swarnika*

These fourteen sonnets in this book
Birthed life in fourteen lines;
Alive, it opened eyes to look
Murderers being built shrines.

.

Chaotic as it might seem to one
Beautiful flowers bloom here;
The spear of Karma spares none
Vultures fated the life of a mare.

.

A rose is radiantly dressed
In petals and thorns alike;
To the eye, the petals impressed
And the thorns waited to strike.

.

Beware! The riots might commence soon.
The ink of the seven poets sustains, a boon!

Featured Poets

Swarnika

Nishtha Trehan

Putul Mangni Mandal

Deepanshi Ailawadi

Gauri Shukla

Khushi Kaushik

Raman Singh

Sonnets

A sonnet can be described as a poem written in fourteen lines with a pre-decided rhyming scheme. Some sonnets are written in a single stanza while others might have about four as well. Many poets have written sonnets in iambic pentameter. However, some have been constructed differently. They might include Alexandria, trochaic meter, volta, among others.

The three major kinds of sonnets are-

- Petrarchan Sonnets
- Shakespearean Sonnets
- Spenserian Sonnets

Sonnets On Life

Sonnets On Life is a beautifully and uniquely designed collection of sonnets. The seven poets, who have contributed to this collection, have presented two sonnets each. There are fourteen sonnets in this collection, just like the number of lines in a sonnet. These sonnets are written on the idea and understanding of Life by these poets. They have expressed themselves in various ways and have portrayed how they resonate with life. While reading this collection, you'd come across different ideas and different expressions. Some of them are contemplative while some of these are a medium to vent out the bursting and culminating emotions. We perceive life in different ways. We live our lives differently. This anthology helps the reader to comprehend the poets and their mindset. An additional sonnet is written in the form of the prologue of this anthology.

Swarnika

Swarnika is an avid reader and an ambivert. She is a glass-half-full kind of a person, not because she is always an optimist but because she believes that a glass that is full has no more scope and ends up creating the most amount of spills.

She completed her Bachelor's and Master's degree from the University of Delhi. She has completed her three-level professional certification in Spanish from Valencia Polytechnic University, Spain. She has also completed her certificate program in French from St. Stephen's College, University of Delhi. She is currently pursuing a Post-Graduate Diploma in Business Administration from Symbiosis Centre for Distance Learning, Pune. She is working on her thesis and research papers to earn her Ph.D. degree in English Literature.

She has a keen interest in criminology and detective fiction. Writings that indulge mystery and rationale speak volumes to her. She has earned her TEFL and TESOL certificates as an English language teacher. She is also a certified dance teacher with specializations in Bharatnatyam, Kathak, and Contemporary. She is also certified in Classical Music and Fine Arts.

She exhibits abundant admiration for food and would call herself a foodie. She believes in living in the moment rather than giving the moment the opportunity to live through you without you even realizing it. She has started her company- Nrityangana Kala Kendra OPC Private Limited on her own. She has been tutoring kids along with mentoring graduate and postgraduate students in academic and creative writing.

On some days she is a dreamer while on others she is a realist. She firmly believes in humanism. Nature mesmerizes her. On a usual day, you'd find her curled up in a corner either with a book or watching a movie/episode while relishing food.

She has initiated this project and has edited the book along with compiling it.

1. Raindrops That Burn

- Swarnika

I held my hand out of the window
To let the raindrops settle in my palm;
Trying to create a home for them, even though
My abode has recently been void of calm.

.

The drops easing in the warmth of my skin
Create an illusion of streams on these lines;
Suppressing the hurricane of emotions within
Fate sealed in those dark and lonely mines.

.

And as another drop falls down,
It instead rolls down my cheek;
I cry and laugh at the same time like a clown,
The clouds join in, bursting lie a pipe on leak.

.

Perhaps the sky empathizes and joins in;
Or it, like the rest, is mocking me within.

2. Carved With Curves

- ***Swarnika***

I was a kid back then who loved to smile.
Finding joy in the little things; such a shame
That pretty curve- I haven't seen in a while.
Once so bright, now dimmed like a dame.
Today the beauty of that curve seems sterile;
Too conscious of the other curves of my frame.

.

"You should lose some pounds", "you look so small!"
"You're too skinny", "those heels make you look too tall!"

.

Why was I carved with these curves?
Why instead of brains, these looks define my worth?
Why these looks presume what one deserves?
Why is my intelligence supposedly suppressed by girth?
Do we realize the horror this society serves?
Eve's apple wasn't worth doing this to the earth...

Nishtha Trehan

Nishtha Trehan is a student at Atma Ram Sanatan Dharma College, University of Delhi, studying English Honours. In her breaks, she likes to read, write, and journal. It is under the guidance of her supervisor, Swarnika Singh, that she has been able to finish this research paper. The sonnets are an attempt to reflect on the different facets of life, focusing primarily on the stage of motherhood, death, and regret.

3. Could have, did not

- Nishtha Trehan

Ink-stained pages breathe words now blurred
Flowers pressed eons ago, thorns reminiscent of an old wound
Blood flows, ghosts of the past stirred
Invoking my name, telling me I'm doomed.

.

I lament the decisions made in my youth,
Innocent wiles pricking at my now old soul
Uncertainty ebbs and fear follows, unveiling the truth
As death stands looming beside, waiting for a stroll.

.

I shut the book, pushing away the grief I endure
As regret claws at the armour I tore before,
Shakily lifting a photograph, I insure
My last moments are spent gazing at a daughter no more.
Invocation to God for a gentle embrace
And for a life next time where I take up space.

4. Circle of Life: one comes, one goes

- Nishtha Trehan

What was once a destination on a horizon uncharted
Arrived with a pair of expectant eyes, her finger seemingly liminal in my hand
As if a single star in a constellation twinkling in the sky had departed
Silence is broken as I witness her eyes expand.

.

The hospital room with its dingy and drab walls she aims to explore
A depressing shade of cream, the room is rejuvenated
With this incandescent being I bore,
Her grandmother's hands turn to rest on my shoulder and suddenly all calm is abated.

.

Growth and decay, contrast each other
Wrinkled, a life lived, against a life so delicate
A lesson of life and what it is to be a mother
Terror of losing one and of not being one would emanate.
Taxing, to make the most of the time I'm given

A battle is waged, against life's transition.

Putul Mangni Mandal

Living in New Delhi, Putul Mangni Mandal was born in December 1996. It is a pseudonym that she has adopted for the literary world. By root, her family comes from Bihar and as mentioned in the name, she belongs to the Mandal community. However, she abhors rigid statism or communism. Putul (meaning doll; it is her mother's pet name) lives with her small family of four. Financially, she is lower middle class. She studied in a government school named Sarvodaya Co. Ed. Senior Secondary in Nanak Pura. She has done her Post Graduation in English from Delhi University and aspires to become a professional writer, too, among many other possible-impossible things.

Poems have fascinated her ever since she read Kanyadan, a poem by the famous romantic Hindi writer Suryakant Tripathi 'Nirālā' in tenth grade. But she never knew that she could write until the day when her teacher Minakshi Mehta asked the whole class to create something. She composed her first poem Lakshya. Since then, she has written many poems. Some of her English poems include On a Bus, Chores, Substitute, My Days, At Last, A Signal, and many others. She also writes in Hindi/Urdu and some of them are Intezar, Upar-Neechey, Bheetar, Chal, etc.

Fingers crossed, she hopes to soon come up with her poem collection. Not limiting herself to poems only, she has initiated in

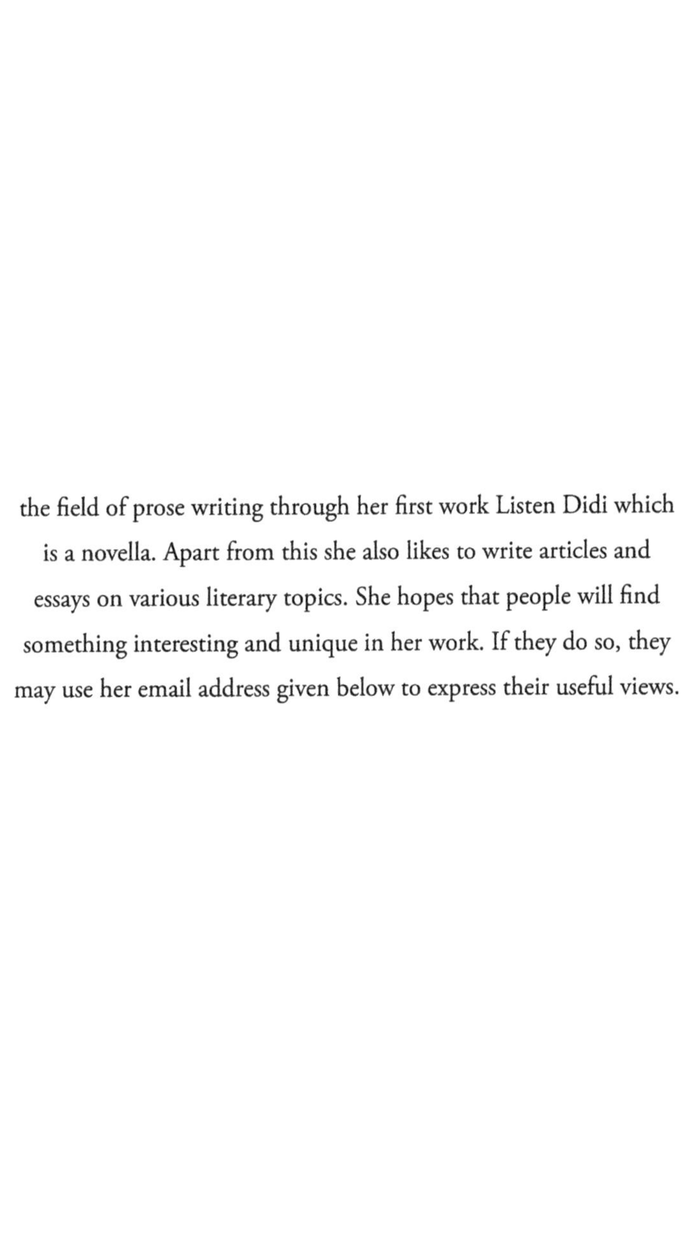

the field of prose writing through her first work Listen Didi which is a novella. Apart from this she also likes to write articles and essays on various literary topics. She hopes that people will find something interesting and unique in her work. If they do so, they may use her email address given below to express their useful views.

5. My Days

- Putul Mangni Mandal

Nights are running after my days
And the days are after my nights
Tedious winds for a cyclone unite
While I become a perplexing bay.

.

They remain consistently the same.
The same they remain, consistently.
Remain, they're same, consistently.
Consistently the same, they remain.

.

And I hold for my dear, dear existence—
Tightly onto the step of the doorway
Radio is gurgling— "inside must I stay
Till the storm dies; carry on resistance"

.

But days still follow nights, nights — my days,
And for now in my life, this dreary circle stays.

6. Unfinished Poems

- Putul Mangni Mandal

Often I hear some of my unfinished poems
Buried in the last pages of my notebooks
Asking to finish at last the finished unfinished
Or to lay a flower at their tomb and look.

.

But I refrain; refrain from ever looking back!
For we shared no relevance if I say the truth
And on the tight supply of reasonable words
Those poor, couldn't grow to grasp their youth.

.

I have moved on to the new hymns and songs!
Life's too short to worry over the leftovers a bit
And if a poem resonates with your loyal soul,
I believe that all the devoted time was worth it.

.

The bruises of the past mistakes will turn into skin,
Remember, you often throw away things to re-fill in.

Deepanshi Ailawadi

Deepanshi Ailawadi holds a Master's degree in English Literature. Since childhood, libraries are her second home, which enable her to travel across time and space. She believes each written page tells a story that should not be left unheard because in the end human beings are made up of little stories stored up in their brain's memory. Writing is one of the mediums through which stories can be heard, touched, and felt. Thus, she decided to write, to pay back her debt to Reading and disseminate stories that have the capability to reform our ways of perception. Writing enables her to hold several personalities and perspectives in her body, sometimes she becomes a bookseller, while other times she becomes a buyer of the book, and sometimes she can be both friend and enemy at once. It is this magic that tempted her to write for others and for herself too.

7. Embrace The Loss

- Deepanshi Ailawadi

Through hidden windows and leaving doors ajar
from our house fallen leaves depart.
Leaving an unannounced war
and a cankering sore on heart.

.

Turning rooms black, unable to look
any corner or seat left by them.
I run to catch them, hold them to a hook,
continue to paste and tape the died stem.

.

My endeavour quiver in vain
as leaves acquired a new home soon.
Soothing my wounds by rain
I realize loss of the serenity of moon.
By one road one gain
and on other left maroon.

8. No One is Complete

- Deepanshi Ailawadi

Some milk, sugar and tea leaves,
makes a wonder, a cup of tea.
Parts making a new whole, this one believes
Is similar to life's key.

.

When I lost, not only I fail
but also my bones were impaired.
When I fall, my skin, hair and nail
too were not willing to be repaired.

.

Neither leaves nor fruit can stand
on a high creeper all alone.
Neither air nor land
can survive without water grown.
Each smallest line in hand
can turn the route of each bone.

Gauri Shukla

Gauri Shukla is a third-year Literature student pursuing her passion for reading and writing from the University of Delhi. President of the Literary Society of the college, she is an avid reader who yearns to get lost in estranged, galvanic worlds of art. A national-level debater, she is someone who doesn't shy away from speaking her mind. An ardent scripturient, she has written articles for The Times of India, The Hindu, The Redstockings Chronicles, etc. She's currently working on a South-Asian anthology as an editor alongside editors from Bangladesh and Pakistan. Her lifelong dream is to document the experiences and sentiments of different people, belonging to different cultures, all around the world. She believes life is too short and time is fleeting thus, each moment needs to be savoured and felt to its optimum level. She likes to describe herself as a wandering cloud that romances with the sky, lost yet free.

9. The Pandora's Curse

- Gauri Shukla

I've spent days wondering
If you ever really wanted me
Stream-like tears cascading,
Into a river destined for the sea.

.

I've written poems filled with metaphors,
I've looked for you in the brightest of places,
Forgot to look in the dark abyss of my heart's remorse.
Oh lord! The place is full of your traces.

.

You opened me up like a Pandora's box, carelessly
The eighth deadly sin forged in the hellfire,
Scissored my guts shamelessly,
Stood unrecognised in the devil's attire.

.

I've wandered long amidst these forlorn shadows,
Wailing and waiting for you by the hallows.

10. A Breath Away

- Gauri Shukla

Love and loss
Mirth and melancholy
A hundred thousand flaws,
In people's personality.

.

Like a pendulum oscillating to and fro
Life is a temporary illusion, a detached dream.
Like the waves crashing on the grainy shore
Life is but a box of chocolates, vanilla, mint or cream.

.

What is life but the time between a single breath
One second, there's air and the next second
There's darkness shed
It's a mean and unfair trade, I reckon.

.

But one's got to live fair and dare themselves each day
For life happens once and then you're on the other side's bay.

Khushi Kaushik

Khushi Kaushik, the elder child in a nuclear family, was born and brought up in Faridabad, Haryana. She studied in DAV Public School, Sec-14, Faridabad, and was good in studies since childhood. She has a keen interest in studying literature. The author of 'Secret of room 333' is known for her flash fiction. She started writing her first book when she was 13, which is a very young age, her interest developed in the field of content writing and she started to write poems, stories and finally decided to write fiction. She is 20 at present and is pursuing English literature from the University of Delhi. Apart from being an author, she is a poetess as well and her compilation of romantic poems 'Shades of love' had a great readership. She is an eager learner and has various interests. She has a keen interest in art, she has been painting since childhood and is a very good singer as well and also has won competitions in singing. She has a dynamic personality and is someone who loves to take up new challenges and broaden her horizons.

11. Living on Strings

- Khushi Kaushik

Aren't we all caged?
Caged and a little raged
Raged because of our anguish
And end up being languish

.

Aren't we all controlled?
Controlled and thus we behold
Behold a part of ourselves
And always hide in provided cells

.

But most of all
Aren't we all
Just done and tired of ourselves?
And need to discover a new self?

.

Because we are just puppets
pouring our sorrow in couplets.

12. Persona

*- **Khushi Kaushik***

Everything falls apart, the heart cannot hold
Misery and sadness are loosened upon the world
The illusionary tide is flooding everywhere
All we can feel is misery here and there.

.

There is absolutely no sense alive in us
And we're afraid to express and be righteous,
We want to but can't go back to starts,
'Coz we're surrounded by brains and not hearts.

.

So we choose to put sufferings safe in hiding
And go unnoticed and enjoy our riding
But we are only humans and not perfect strategist
And thus the deuteragonist abruptly turns into a protagonist.

.

And from what I've learned is this feeling,
The livings are dead and the dead are living.

Raman Singh

Raman Singh was born in the year 2001 in Haryana, India. He never did things to pass time, when he held on to a thing, he gave himself completely to it. May it be playing basketball for nine years, may it be doing theatre, which also induced interest in literature. He is currently pursuing a BA(Hons) in English, from Delhi University, and is an important part of the theatre society. He has also acted in six theatrical productions and has written several short plays and stories. Not to forget his love for Hindi Literature, which has added new dimensions to his imaginations and in which he finds those values and thoughts which otherwise would've been too late to discover. If there is anything else that he loves, that is a cup of coffee. His notion of feeling content and happy is to have a cup of coffee with a brownie while reading a book.

13. Unparalleled Life

- Raman Singh

Oh life! why are you a circle?
Why do I return there from where I departed
Everyday you throw a new hurdle
And then ask me why am I startled
I who thought would jump like a rabbit comes to know that I am a mere turtle
And then not being able to jump, I am seen as retarded
Isn't this unfair that you with your controller encircle?
And then are you happy to see me martyred?

.

Why aren't you a square, triangle, rhombus or a rectangle?
Why do you want yourself to be centered?
Why aren't you a straight line with a one-eightydegree angle?
Why can't I leave after being entered?
Why cannot we be two parallel lines with an undefined angle?
That I can learn without being mentored.

14. Like Everyday

- Raman Singh

Woke up like every day at five today
Brushed my teeth, washed my body, changed my clothes and was ready
Like everyday cooked an omelette for breakfast today
Went to work, finished pending work, shouted at my junior the shout of my boss and left the office in a hurry
Like everyday came home at six today
Changed my clothes, ate a protein bar and for the evening jog was ready
Like everyday came back exactly at eight today
Took bath, wore nightwear, and headed to the kitchen to cook spaghetti
Like everyday finished eating by nine-thirty today
Watched television, drank a glass of milk, and made the schedule for tomorrow which was fixed already
Like everyday layed down on the bed by ten-thirty today
Wrapped the blanket, adjusted the pillow and closed my eyes heavy

.

Like everyday I wasted today

Like everyday I repeated today.

The Patterns Of These Rhymes

Swarnika

Prologue

ABAB CDCD EFEF GG

Raindrop That Burn

ABAB CDCD EFEF GG

Carved With Curves

ABABAB CC DEDEDE

Nishtha Trehan

Could have, did not

ABAB CDCD EFEF GG

Circle of Life: one comes, one goes

ABAB CDCD EFEF GG

Putul Mangni Mandal

My Days

ABBA CDDC EFFE GG

Unfinished Poems

ABCB DEFE GHIH JJ

Deepanshi Ailawadi

Embrace The Loss

ABAB CDCD EFEFEF

No One Is Complete

ABAB CDCD EFEFEF

Gauri Shukla

The Pandora's Curse

ABAB CDCD EFEF GG

A Breath Away

ABAB CDCD EFEF GG

Khushi Kaushik

Living on Strings

AABB CCDD EEFF GG

Persona

AABB CCDD EEFF GG

Raman Singh

Unparalleled Life

ABABABAB CDCDCD

Like Everyday

ABABABABABAB AA

Thank You!

Dear Reader,

Thank you for reading this collection of sonnets. We sincerely hope you've enjoyed the work. If you've any feedback that you'd like to share with us, kindly reach out to us via swara@nrityanganakalakendra.com. We'll definitely revert.

Regards,

Swarnika

Nrityangana Kala Kendra

9 798886 064254

Printed by Libri Plureos GmbH in Hamburg,
Germany